21st Century Junior Library

Diplodocus

by Josh Gregory

CHERRY LAKE PUBLISHING * ANN ARBOR, MICHIGAN

Published in the United States of America by Cherry Lake Publishing
Ann Arbor, Michigan
www.cherrylakepublishing.com

Content Adviser: Gregory M. Erickson, PhD, Dinosaur Paleontologist, Department of Biological Science, Florida State University, Tallahassee, Florida

Reading Adviser: Marla Conn, ReadAbility, Inc.

Photo Credits: Cover, ©Mark Boulton/Alamy; Pages 4, 6, 8, 12, 14, and 16, ©Catmando/Shutterstock, Inc.; page 10, ©Linda Bucklin/Shutterstock, Inc.; page 18, ©Michael Rosskothen/Shutterstock, Inc.; page 20, ©Presselect/Alamy.

LIBRARY OF CONGRESS CATALOGING-IN-PUBLICATION DATA
Gregory, Josh.
  Diplodocus/by Josh Gregory.
    p. cm.—(21st century junior library. Dinosaurs and prehistoric animals)
  Summary: "Learn about the incredible dinosaur known as Diplodocus"—Provided by publisher.
  Audience: K to grade 3.
  Includes bibliographical references and index.
  ISBN 978-1-62431-165-9 (lib. bdg.)—ISBN 978-1-62431-231-1 (e-book)—
ISBN 978-1-62431-297-7 (pbk.)
  1. Diplodocus—Juvenile literature. 2. Dinosaurs—Juvenile literature. I. Title.
  QE862.S3G767 2014
  567.913—dc23   2013004807

Cherry Lake Publishing would like to acknowledge the work of The Partnership for 21st Century Skills.
Please visit www.p21.org *for more information.*

Printed in the United States of America
Corporate Graphics Inc.
July 2013
CLFA11

CONTENTS

Many scientists believe *Diplodocuses*
lived in herds.

What Was Diplodocus?

Have you ever seen a giraffe at the zoo? Imagine if its tail were even longer than its neck. It would look a lot like the dinosaur *Diplodocus*! *Diplodocus* lived between 154 and 150 million years ago. Like all dinosaurs, it is now **extinct**.

A *Diplodocus*'s tail was long and very heavy.

The name *Diplodocus* comes from Greek words meaning "double **beam**." *Diplodocus* was given this name because it had two rows of bones underneath its tail. These bones helped support the weight of the massive tail.

Think!

Why did *Diplodocus* need extra bones to support its tail? Have you seen any other animal with such a big tail? What would it feel like to carry such a big tail?

Diplodocus may have eaten water plants that grew around lakes and swamps.

Diplodocus lived mainly in what is now western North America. This area was warmer when *Diplodocus* lived than it is today. It was also wetter. This weather helped many different kinds of plants grow. *Diplodocus* had plenty to eat!

Diplodocus's tail could be almost twice
as long as its neck.

What Did *Diplodocus* Look Like?

Diplodocus was one of the largest dinosaurs. A fully grown *Diplodocus* was usually about 85 feet (26 meters) long. Some could grow even longer! These huge dinosaurs weighed around 18 tons. That is about as heavy as six cars!

Diplodocus had a very small brain for an animal its size.

Diplodocus had a huge body. But its head was very small. It also had a very small brain. This means it was not a very smart dinosaur.

Diplodocus's **skull** had a long shape. It had long front teeth and no back teeth.

Diplodocus had large feet with five toes, just like modern elephants.

Diplodocus had wide legs to support its huge body. It had long back legs and shorter front legs. Its shoulders were closer to the ground than its back end was. Each leg ended in a wide foot. Each foot had five toes.

Create!

Try making a model of *Diplodocus* out of clay. Be sure to shape its long neck and tail. Give it big legs to keep it from falling over!

Diplodocus's long neck may have helped it reach leaves high in trees.

How Did *Diplodocus* Live?

Diplodocus was a **herbivore**. It used its front teeth to bite leaves from plants. *Diplodocus* did not have any back teeth. It probably swallowed its food without chewing. Scientists are not sure which plants it ate. It may have reached into the treetops for leaves. It may also have eaten plants that grew on the ground.

Diplodocus could use its heavy body and big feet
to scare or hurt an enemy.

Dinosaurs like *Allosaurus* were **predators**. They sometimes hunted *Diplodocus*. *Diplodocus* was not always an easy target. It could defend itself by swinging its powerful tail. It could also stomp on predators with its heavy feet.

Museums such as the Natural History Museum in London, England, have *Diplodocus* skeletons on display.

Scientists study dinosaurs and other extinct animals by looking at **fossils**. A scientist named Samuel Williston found the first *Diplodocus* fossils in 1877. Scientists have discovered only a few *Diplodocus* skeletons since then. But these few fossils have taught us a lot!

Make a Guess!

Why is it so unusual to find *Diplodocus* fossils? Think about where fossils are found. Why might it be difficult to look for them? A teacher or librarian can help you find the answer.

GLOSSARY

beam (BEEM) a long, thick piece of material, such as wood or metal, used as a support in a building

extinct (ik-STINGKT) describing a type of plant or animal that has completely died out

fossils (FAH-suhlz) the preserved remains of living things from thousands or millions of years ago

herbivore (HUR-buh-vor) an animal that eats only plants

predators (PRED-uh-turz) animals that live by hunting other animals for food

skull (SKUHL) the bones that make up an animal's head

FIND OUT MORE

BOOKS

Dodson, Peter. *Diplodocus Up Close: Long-Necked Dinosaur.* Berkeley Heights, NJ: Baily Books/ Enslow Elementary, 2011.

Rockwood, Leigh. *Diplodocus.* New York: PowerKids Press, 2012.

WEB SITES

Diplodocus: Facts About the Longest Dinosaur

www.livescience.com /24326-diplodocus.html Read more on *Diplodocus* and check out photos of *Diplodocus* fossils.

Science Kids: Diplodocus Facts for Kids

www.sciencekids.co.nz /sciencefacts/dinosaurs /diplodocus.html Check out some fun facts about *Diplodocus.*

INDEX

ABOUT THE AUTHOR

Josh Gregory writes and edits books for kids. He lives in Chicago, Illinois.